101 THINGS women WANT *from* THEIR men

Compiled by
Annette Bridges

Illustrated by
Lesley Vernon

Designed by
Janie Owen-Bugh

Illustrated by Lesley Vernon
www.lvdesignhouse.com

Layout and Cover Design by Janie Owen-Bugh
www.janieowenbugh.com

Printed in the United States of America.

ISBN: 978-1-946371-48-5

To my darling husband,
John, who loves me unconditionally
and tries really hard to please me.
Your efforts to understand me are
very much appreciated!

Introduction

I didn't set out to write a book that would proclaim to the world what women want from their men. I mean, who the heck am I to presume to know what every woman wants. What I want these days at sixty-something is quite different from what I thought I wanted forty years ago. So I'm not suggesting that all women at every age and stage in life want the same things.

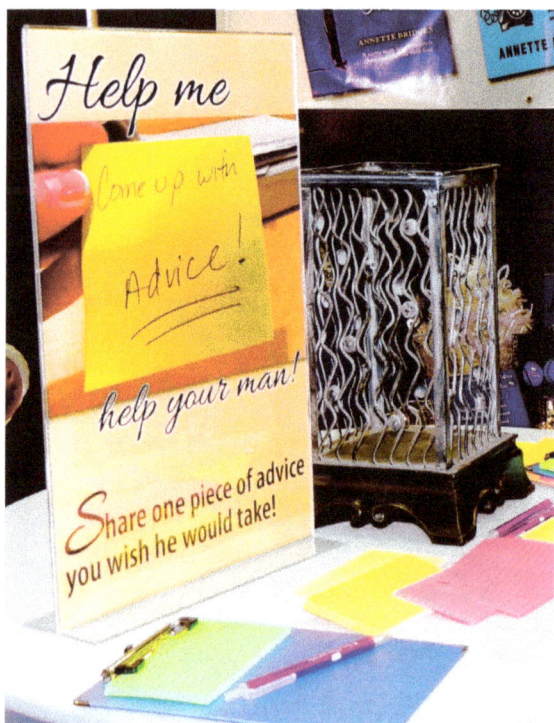

How did this book come about?

At a women's conference in 2013, I was a speaker and exhibitor shortly after my first two books were published. I thought it might be a lively conversational activity to ask booth visitors an engaging question. In particular, I asked women: "What's one piece of advice you would like to give your man?" (And yes, my intention at the time was to be sassy and satirical.) I created a table display that had this question big and bold on a colorful sign and provided women with index cards and pens to write their answers and drop them in a container.

My idea proved to be a good one.

No woman could walk by my sign without a smile, and most all were anxious to answer its question. I enjoyed both hearing and reading what women had to say. Women freely shared what they wanted and what they didn't want. They revealed what they needed and what they didn't need. They gave advice, and they gave admonitions. There were giggles, but there were also some tears. There were women who conveyed their fear to be upfront and honest about their wants and needs because they were afraid their man might dismiss them as insignificant.

There were women who expressed similar wishes and longings. You'll probably notice quite a few tips regarding listening, including why to listen, when to listen, and how to listen.

Some women's answers were shared with sarcasm.

However, even those suggested a very real underlying desire. I'm pretty sure there was always a serious reason for what one of my sisters was saying, in spite of how she said it.

So trust me, guys, when your woman speaks, there is truth in those words and a real yearning hidden somewhere between the lines.

You'll notice each piece of advice is framed in quotation marks because the advice is not mine. You are truly reading the eclectic collection of comments written and voiced by the variety of women who visited my conference booth.

This book is not trying to speak for all women.

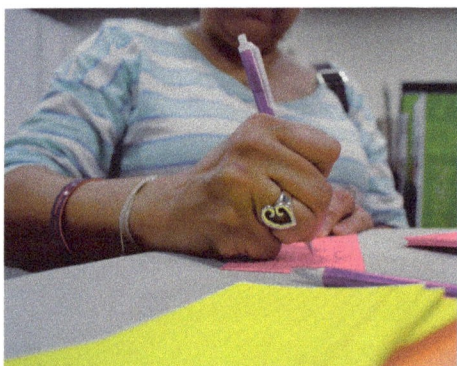

And it's certainly not meant to suggest that men don't care about or are not interested in the feelings and needs of women. After forty-plus years of marriage to my man, I know there are men who absolutely want to please their women. I know because I married one of them!

The truth is, none of us are mind readers. We don't know what our partners are thinking or feeling unless they tell us or we ask. And then we must be willing to listen and try to understand what is being said. It's not our place to agree or disagree with how another feels. We only need to acknowledge, accept, and respect that their feelings are theirs.

After I poured over all of the women's comments

from my fun question, I felt what they were saying was too important to keep to myself. So I decided to publish them and share them with you. My hope is that this little book will spark some healthy dialogue between couples. There is much good advice in these 101 wants that is applicable to both partners in a relationship. Being willing to hear, and in this case read, what some women said they want and don't want from their men may be a good place to begin a discussion to consider what each of you wants or doesn't want in your own partnership.

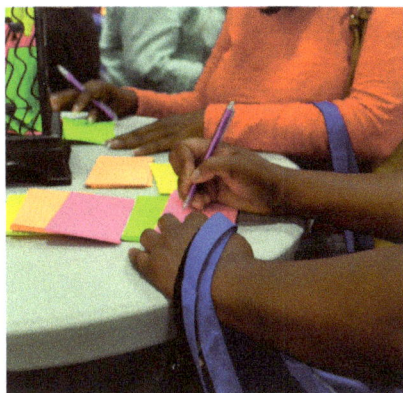

If you're a man wondering whether this is a book for you, the fact you're wondering says you have a vested interest in pleasing and understanding your mate. I sincerely applaud you. Clearly, you care about what your woman wants and needs.

And if you're a woman, I suspect there will be wants shared by other women that resonate with you. You may laugh in agreement with some of them, and others may be more sobering. In some ways, this book represents the sisterhood talking to each other.

During the process of organizing, I found I could group and categorize the 101 wants into eight sections, which are outlined in the Table of Contents.

So fellas, if you want to really know what women want, this book was designed especially for you, written collectively by hundreds of women who wanted you to know.

Table of Contents

always,
ALWAYS,
always...

1

"Always be **honest.**"

2

"ALWAYS SMELL good."

3

"Always SAY yes!"

4

Put the seat down! ALWAYS!

5

ALWAYS

take the time

to let me know

THAT I AM

important

and that you care.

6

"Always **back me** *in front of* THE KIDS —or anyone."

7

"**No matter HOW** long *we've been together,* **ALWAYS** take me *on special* **DATES.**"

8

Notice

when you've

hurt my feelings, and

DO SOMETHING

ABOUT IT.

ALWAYS!

THE **why,**
WHEN,
and **HOW**
of listening...

9

"**TRY**
really hard
to hear **AND**
UNDERSTAND
what I'M
saying."

10

"listen *and please* **TRY NOT** to pass JUDGMENT."

11

"**LISTEN**
and acknowledge
my presence."

12

"**YOU MAY THINK** you know what *I'm going to say,* BUT YOU DON'T. **KEEP LISTENING** *and don't cut me off.*"

13

PLEASE *pay attention* **WHEN** I'm talking to you.

14

"Listen *and* **value** WHAT I SAY."

15

"ADJUST *your* selective hearing."

16

"Listening is a TWO-WAY STREET. If you **WANT** to be **HEARD,** don't forget to **RETURN** the FAVOR."

17

If you **DIDN'T** HEAR what I SAID, *don't* **PRETEND** that *you* did.

18

"SMILE
and listen *quietly.*
GIVE A *small* gesture
OR NOD.
Answer *with a soft* **VOICE**
and say, 'OKAY.'"

19

" Listen *more* **to what** I WANT. "

never...
stop...
DON'T...

20

DON'T assume
you KNOW
WHAT I NEED
or how
I feel.

21

"STOP procrastinating."

22

"Stop **FREAKING OUT** *when I* **come TO YOU** *with* questions **OR ISSUES.**"

23

"STOP TAKING me FOR granted. COOKING, CLEANING, DOING the LAUNDRY, and grocery shopping are NOT my jobs."

24

"NEVER, ever LIE!"

25

"Never *go to bed* **angry.**"

26

"Don't lie *when you have* ALREADY BEEN **CAUGHT** in a lie."

27

DON'T *record* ANYTHING *you don't want* **anyone** *to* know. **DON'T** *take* PICTURES *you don't want* **anyone** *to* see. **DON'T** *write* ANYTHING *down you don't want* **anyone** *to* read.

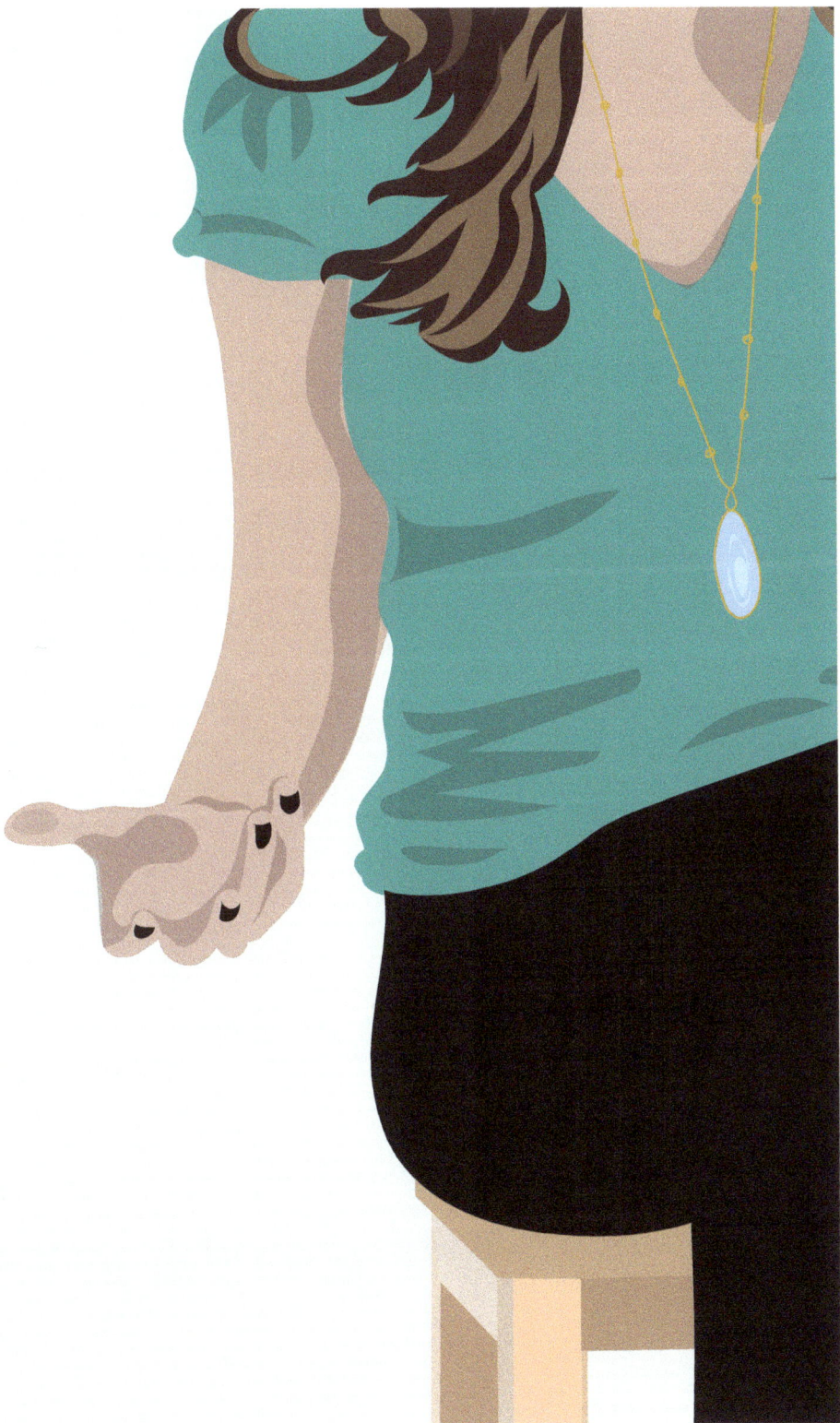

28

"Never **promise** ANYTHING *you can't* follow THROUGH **WITH.**"

29

"**DON'T** complain *about* petty **MONEY** *matters* *when* THEY don't *even* **MATTER.**"

30

" NEVER *tell me* WHAT *to do.* "

31

Stop
BEING
selfish

32

"NEVER forget
I have **feelings.**
Be sensitive *to*
WHAT *you* SAY *and*
HOW *you* SAY IT."

33

"Don't **TRY** *to* **OUTDO** me."

34

STOP
complaining.

35

DON'T
watch
too much
television.99

affection
and SEX...

36

"**Listen**
to my needs
IN THE BEDROOM.
TREAT ME
before yourself!"

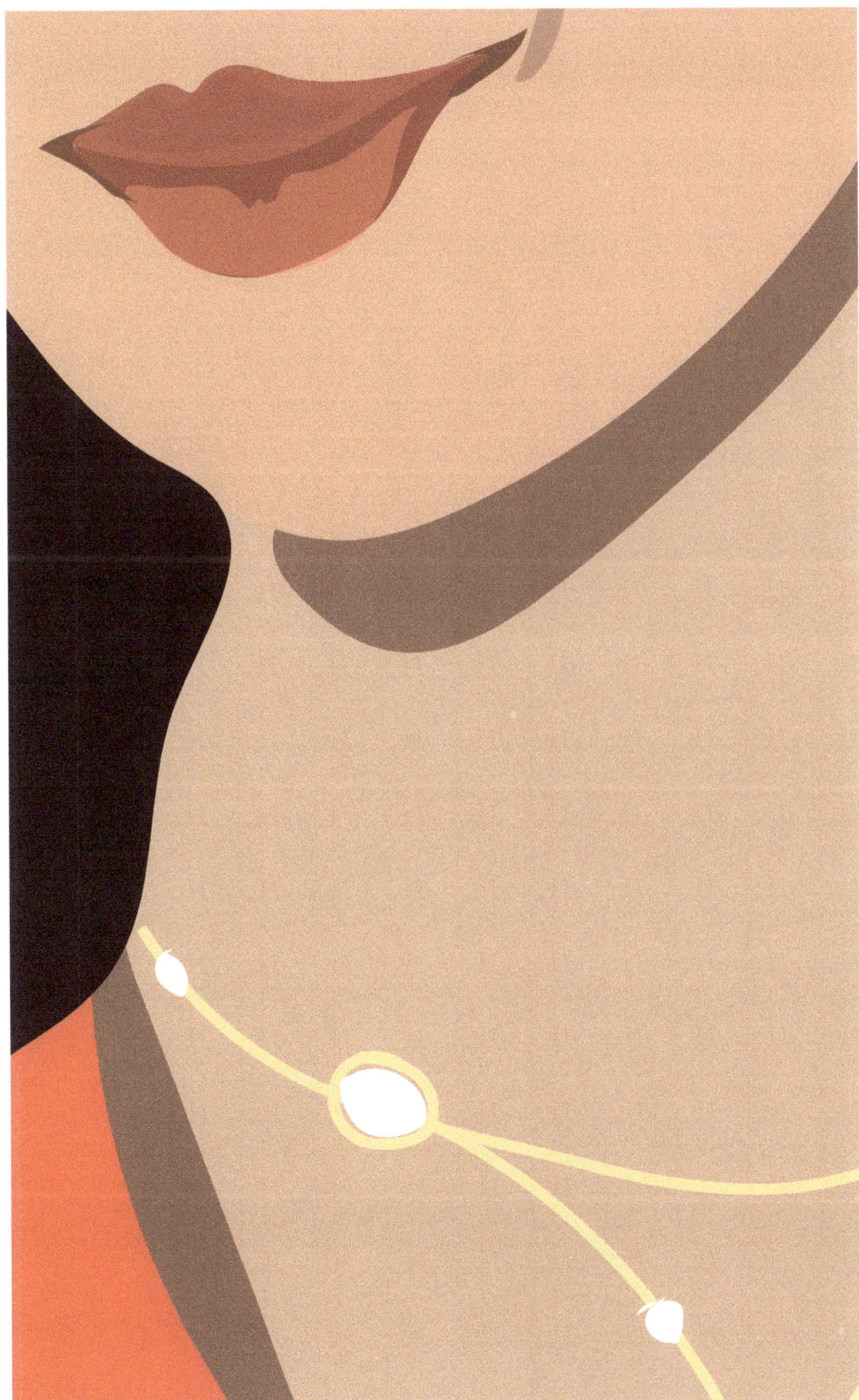

37

"When *I'm* tired, **wash** *the* **dishes!** YOU'LL *be* AMAZED *at* how **MUCH** more **interested** I WILL BE IN **SEX.**"

38

"You *can't* be grumpy *with me* ALL DAY LONG **AND THEN** *turn on* *the* **CHARM** *at* *ten o'clock and expect* **anything!!**"

39

"**Hold my hand.**
It means a lot!
Be passionate.
BE AFFECTIONATE.
BE ROMANTIC."

40

Hug *and* kiss *me*
AT OTHER TIMES
besides *when*
we are
in the bed.

ALL
actions
matter...

41

"Help clean up
AFTER MEALS."

42

WHEN YOU
wash the dishes,
it means also
CLEANING THE
kitchen counter.

P.S. Pans are also dishes.

43

"Taking me
TO DINNER
DOES NOT
count as a
birthday present."

44

"DO THINGS
you **don't like** to do
because THE WOMAN
you **LOVE**
WOULD LIKE
to do **them.**"

45

Wash DISHES
AT LEAST
once a week.

46

When *I'm* crying
FROM A **bad day**,
I just need you to
hug me
AND LISTEN!

47

"Be willing
TO LEARN HOW
to **dance** *with me.*
TRY NEW
things *with* me."

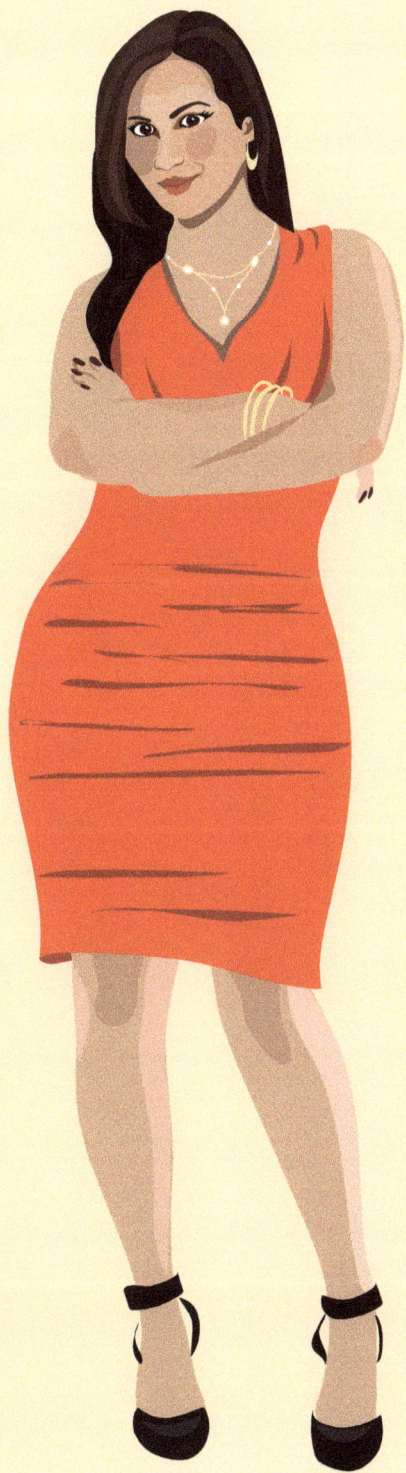

48

"Give me
YOUR TIME AND
attention."

49

IF YOU SEE *something* *that* **NEEDS** TO BE DONE, **don't ask,** just do it.

50

CLEAN UP
AFTER
yourself.

51

"Be thoughtful. SHOW *your* **appreciation.** *Say* THANK YOU."

52

Pick up
your
DAMN socks!

53

"DO THE dishes *when* I cook."

54

"TAKE ME shopping. IT MAKES ME feel special TO YOU."

55

Help with
HOUSEWORK.
Be a team player.
DO YOUR
PART!

56

Treat me

SPECIAL.

DON'T BE SO

domineering.

57

"*Be a* gentleman.
OPEN DOORS.
Have **good
manners.**"

58

"SPOIL ME!"

59

"**GIVE ME**
WHAT I LIKE
without me
having
to **ASK.**"

60

"Treat the one
YOU LOVE
like you **treat**
your **FRIENDS.**"

61

"Be patient
with me."

62

Put down
THE VIDEO
GAMES.

63

"I want you *to* **want** *to* DO THINGS *with me,* **NOT** BECAUSE *you* **HAVE** *to.*"

communication
counts...

64

"Communicate!"

65

"WHEN I SAY **'nothing'** *when you ask what's wrong,* I REALLY MEAN **something** *is on my mind, and* **I need you** *to* care enough *to keep* *asking* QUESTIONS."

66

Learn *how to*
EFFECTIVELY
COMMUNICATE
with me *by*
BEING OPEN
and **honest.**

67

"*Be more*
understanding
and
compassionate."

68

"*It's* okay *to* **share** *your worries,* **FEARS,** *and* DOUBTS with me."

69

"Think *before* YOU SPEAK, *and* choose WORDS *that are* NOT hurtful."

70

When you want *my* help, *explain what you* WANT ME TO DO **before** *we get started,* AND DON'T GET frustrated *with me* *if I don't do* **WHAT YOU** **wanted** *because* *you didn't* tell *me.*

71

Be a good
LISTENER.

72

"**TALK** *with* **ME.**
Engage *in*
CONVERSATION.
Share ideas.
Care about
what I'm thinking."

73

Let's not argue *and* **agree** *to*
DISAGREE.

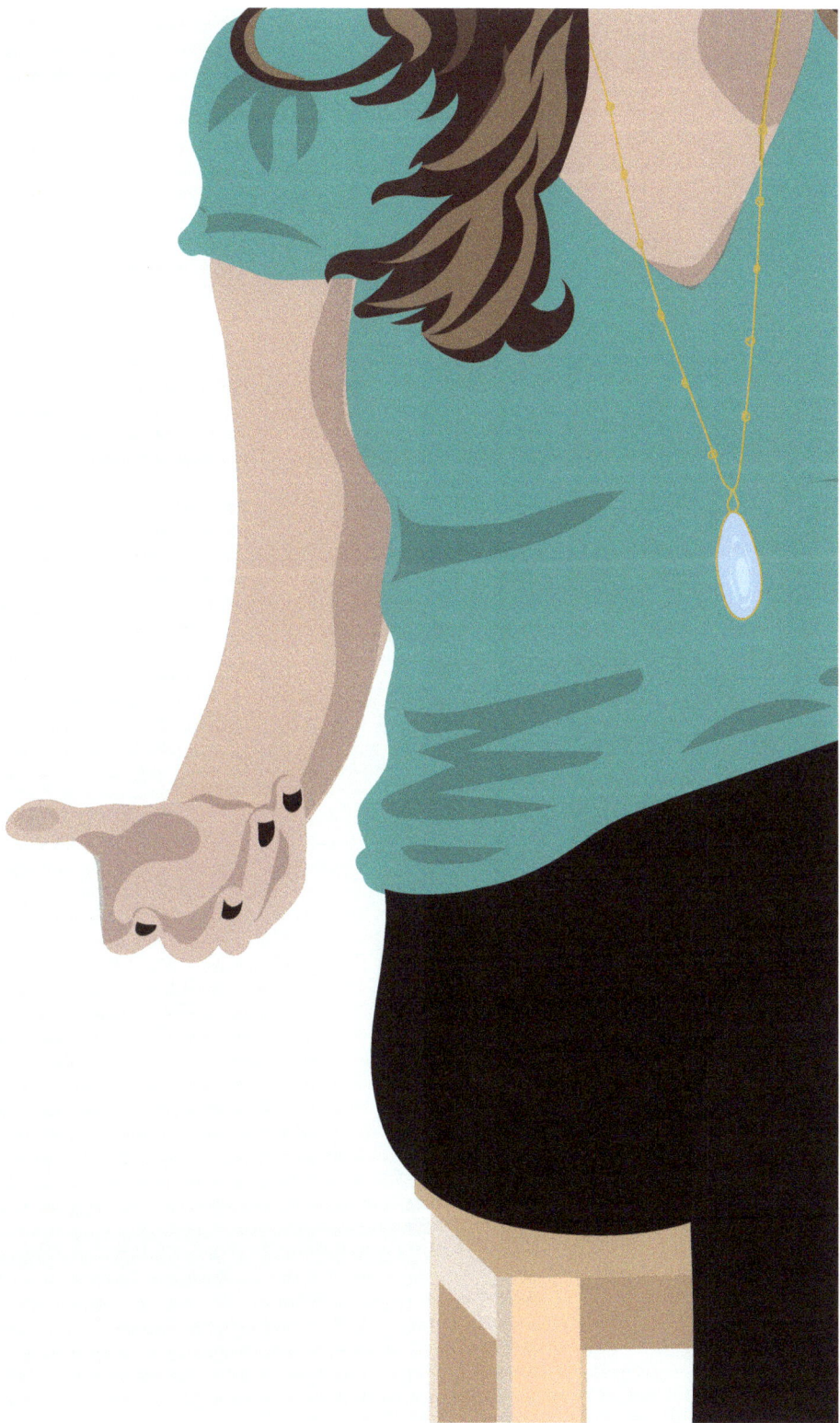

74

" Just apologize! "

75

"Give me encouragement AND POSITIVE SUPPORT. Tell me I CAN do WHATEVER I am TRYING to accomplish."

76

"My ideas *are* IMPORTANT, TOO. **DECISION MAKING** *and* **finances** *are a* **SHARED** responsibility."

77

It's more IMPORTANT *to be* **KIND** THAN *to be* **right.**

78

Understand *that sometimes* women *just need to* VENT *about* SOMETHING *and that the venting* **ALONE** *helps to make us* **FEEL BETTER.** *Stop thinking that* **every problem** *requires an immediate offer of a solution. It is* **MADDENING** *when* *you try to* TELL ME WHAT TO DO *to fix something when* I just want to blow off steam.

wants,
longings,
AND
hopes...

79

"Stay faithful."

80

I NEED *a*
family **man**
who will be a
good
ROLE MODEL
to his children.

81

"YOU MAY *be* king *but* I'M STILL *the* **queen!** **TREAT ME** *with* respect."

82

Learn *that a* **RELATIONSHIP** *is* *a* **TEAM** *effort.*

83

"WHEN YOU ARE *in a* relationship *with someone,* YOU ARE *in* THAT relationship *with* **THAT** **one person** only."

84

"ONE
DIAMOND
is **not** *enough*
FOR A
lifetime."

85

"Get your PRIORITIES **right.**"

86

BE MY
warrior!

87

Respect
ME.

88

"Pamper me with FLOWERS and OTHER love gifts."

89

"Plan **surprise** ROMANTIC getaways."

more **to** REMEMBER...

90

Ask *for*
directions.

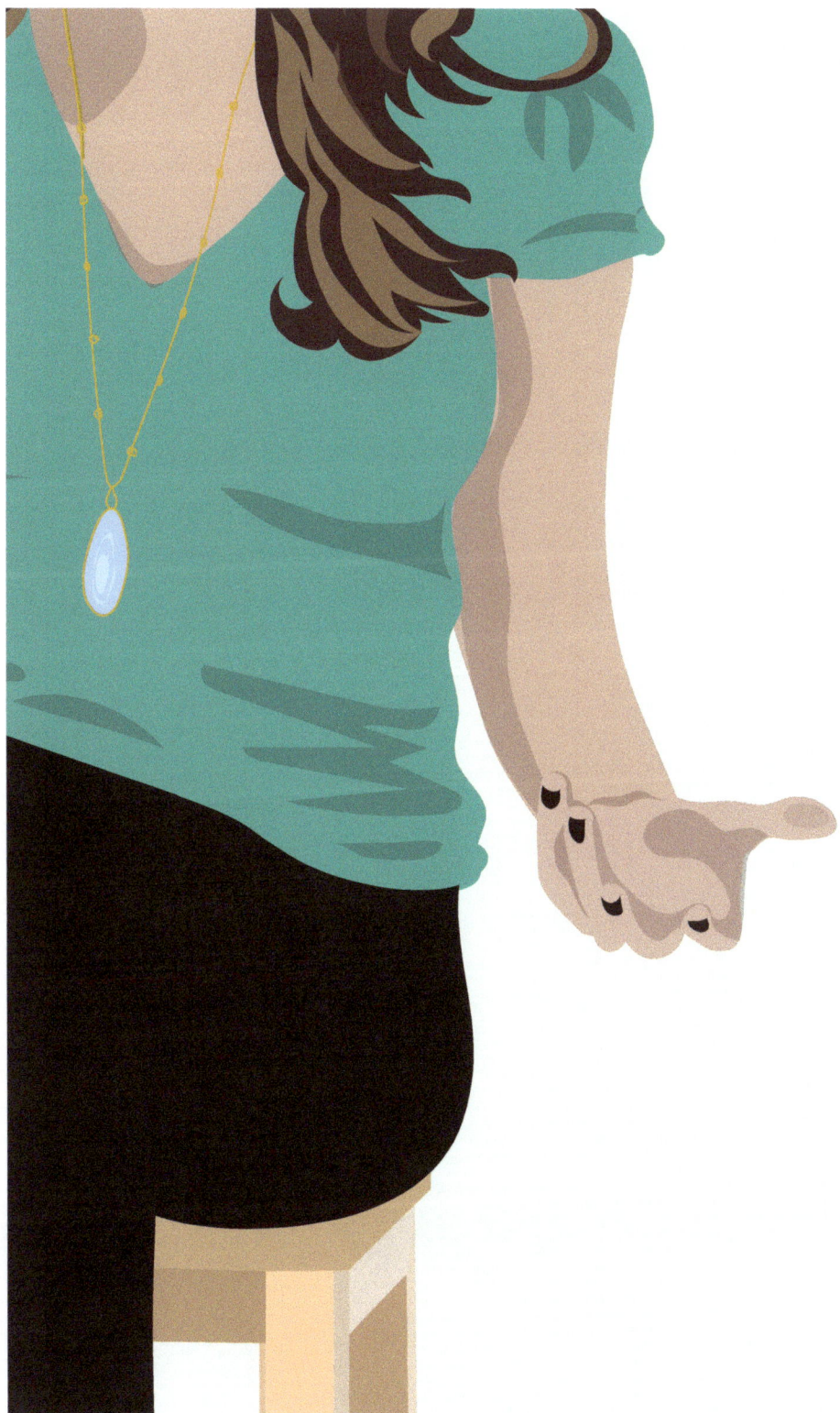

91

"Be a man *of* **integrity.**"

92

"**LISTEN**
TO YOUR
mamma,
who **gave** *you*
GOOD ADVICE."

93

Sometimes **I need** *some* SPACE **AND TO BE** LEFT ALONE *for* **A WHILE.**

94

Take *my*
ADVICE.

95

"Trust me!"

96

Keep a
GOOD JOB.

97

"REMEMBER *that* no MATTER *how* **BAD** *my* family *may* **seem** *to you,* *they* ARE STILL my **FAMILY.**"

98

"Read *the* DIRECTIONS."

99

Don't *ask* 'WHY'
EVERY *time* I GO
do something
I WANT *to* DO.

100

Happy **wife**
=
happy **LIFE.**

101

"**WANT** *to* know WHAT YOUR woman WANTS."

About the author

Annette Bridges is an author and founder of Ranch House Press, a publisher of books, journals, and more that empower, encourage, and entertain. She has published nonfiction books, coloring books, journals, and even a cookbook for children. Before writing books, this former public and homeschool educator spent a decade writing instructive and light-hearted columns for Texas newspapers, magazines, and websites.

Today, Annette writes a monthly Country Lifestyle column titled "When a City Girl Goes Country" for North Texas Farm and Ranch Magazine. She and her husband John are cattle ranchers in north Texas and have been married for over 40 years.

She is also the owner of Ranch House Gift Shop on Etsy and has shop space in downtown Denison, Texas. She uses her art, photography, and the words that are important to her to create all kinds of unique and original products you'll find in her shop. You can learn more about Annette at her website:

www.annettebridges.com

and by following her on Facebook:

@TexasAuthorAnnetteBridges

TOP RIGHT:
Keeping an eye on her man while wrangling cattle on their ranch.

MIDDLE RIGHT:
At her gift shop space in downtown Denison, Texas.

BOTTOM RIGHT:
Driving the tractor.

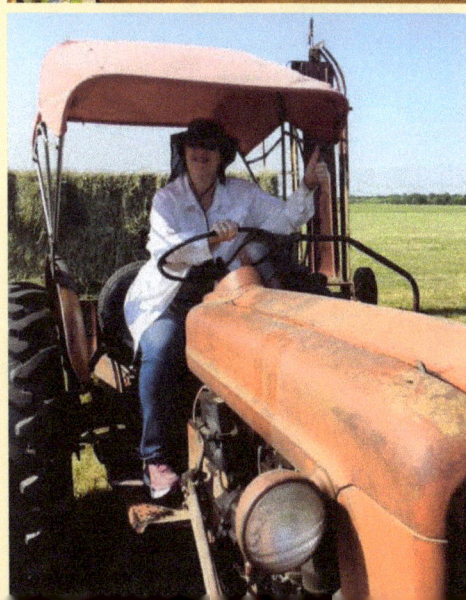

Other Titles by Annette

Mamma Said So 20 pearls of wisdom from a southern sage.

Color-N-Doodle Your World An inspiring collection of coloring pages with your own space to doodle and create.

My Furry Friend A keepsake journal.

A Dachshund Tale Lessons learned from my dog.

Color Your World Journal Series 18 themed journals.

Jot Journals 18 themed pocket-sized journals.

Oh, How the Years Fly By! A whimsical adult coloring book.

Oh, How the Years Fly By! A whimsical inspirational quote book.

The Gospel According to Mamma One mother's philosophy on love, God, money, aging, decisions, change, and much more.

Be Queen of Your Life A savvy mom helps daughters command and rule their lives.

Have Lipstick, Will Travel How to reimagine your life, purpose, and hair color.

Lady and Bella: Totally Different, Totally Friends A coloring storybook for children.

Lady and Bella: Totally Friends Journal Especially for children.

Lady and Bella's Alphabet Kitchen A to Z recipes for kid cooks.

About the graphic designer

Janie Owen-Bugh, a graduate of the Art Institute of Dallas, has made a name for herself with her attention to detail, out-of-the-box ideas, technical savvy, and problem-solving ability. Throughout her career, she has designed for print and digital platforms, as well as video editing for a variety of industries.

It all began with a passion for publishing, building a foundation in multi-page documents such as newsletters, magazines, catalogs, and the like. These days she assists authors with self-publishing, designing dozens of books and over 50 book covers in the process.

Janie lives in a suburb of Dallas, Texas, and enjoys spending time with her two granddaughters, painting, singing, and traveling. She once lived in Honduras doing missionary work and enjoys traveling back there every chance she gets.

To see more of Janie's work, please visit her website at:

janieowenbugh.com

About the illustrator

Lesley Vernon is an illustrator, graphic designer, and fine artist. She has a BA in Fine Arts and is pursuing a Master's degree in Art Therapy, with plans to graduate in 2022. Lesley has illustrated several children's coloring books and created a number of other book designs with Annette Bridges. In addition, Lesley loves drawing in pen & ink and painting with watercolor.

Lesley, along with her husband and two sons, lives in southeastern Massachusetts. She spends her free time hiking in the woods and mountains of New England, walking the dog, knitting, practicing yoga, and raising a flock of backyard chickens. She and her family enjoy being outdoors in all seasons — snowshoeing and skiing in the winter and camping in the summer.

To see more of Lesley's work, please visit her website at:

www.lvdesignhouse.com

www.ingramcontent.com/pod-product-compliance
Lightning Source LLC
Chambersburg PA
CBHW052111030426
42335CB00025B/2936